THE HISTORY DETECTIVE INVESTIGATES

Post-War Britain

Simon Adams

WAYLAND

The History Detective series:
The Celts
Anglo-Saxons
Tudor Exploration
Tudor Home
Tudor Medicine
Tudor Theatre
Tudor War
The Civil Wars
Victorian Crime
Victorian Factory
Victorian School
Victorian Transport
Local History
The Industrial Revolution
Post-War Britain

First published in 2008 by Wayland

Copyright © Wayland 2008

Wayland
338 Euston Road
London NW1 3BH

Wayland Australia
Level 17/207 Kent Street
Sydney, NSW 2000

Editor: Camilla Lloyd
Designer: Simon Burrough
Picture Researcher: Shelley Noronha

Picture Acknowledgments: The author and publisher would like to thank the following for their pictures to be reproduced in this publication: Cover photographs: Main: Alamy: Popperfoto/Alamy, right: Topfoto; Alamy: Popperfoto/Alamy: 7 (t), 14, 15 (t), 19 (t), Helene Rogers/Alamy: 22 (t), Michael Booth/Alamy: 28; AKG: akg-images/ ullstein bild: 17 (t); The Art Archive: John Meek/The Art Archive: 9 (b); Topfoto: 4, 5 (both), 8, 9 (t), 11, 12 (both), 13, 15 (b), 17 (b), 18, 19 (b), 20 (b), 21, 26, 29, AP/Topfoto: 10, 16, 22 (b), Harold Chapman/Topfoto: 20 (t), PA/Topfoto: 25 (both); Wayland Picture Library: 6, 7 (b), 23, 29 (b).

British Library Cataloguing in Publication Data:
  Adams, Simon, 1955-
  Post war Britain. - (The history detective investigates)
  1. Great Britain - History - 20th century – Juvenile literature
  2. Great Britain - Social conditions - 1945-Juvenile literature
  I. Title
  941'.085

ISBN: 978 0 7502 5400 7

Printed in China

Wayland is a division of Hachette Children's Books, an Hachette Livre UK company

Contents

Words in **bold** can be found in the glossary on page 30

The history detective Sherlock Bones, will help you to find clues and collect evidence about Post-War Britain. Wherever you see one of Sherlock's paw-prints, you will find a mystery to solve. The answers can be found on page 31.

Who ran Britain after the war?

In 1945, Britain emerged victorious at the end of World War II. Britain and her allies – the **USA**, the **USSR** (now Russia) and France – had defeated Germany, Italy and Japan. The war had been won, and now it was time to secure peace.

In 1945, Britain was victorious, but it was also **bankrupt**. It had spent all its money on arms and the armed forces. Many of its towns and cities had been bombed and its factories and homes wrecked. The country was exhausted after six years of war and longed to return to a comfortable peace.

The king during the war years was George VI. He had become king when his elder brother Edward VIII unexpectedly abdicated (gave up) his throne in 1936 so that he could marry an American divorcee, Mrs Wallis Simpson. George had not expected to become king and had a terrible stammer that made talking very difficult for him. However, he proved to be a great success. He toured bombed areas with his wife, Queen Elizabeth (the mother of our present queen) and raised morale among both civilians and troops.

The prime minister during the war was Winston Churchill, the leader of the **Conservative Party**. Churchill had led a **coalition** government made up of all the parties since he became prime minister in 1940. He was a brilliant war leader, whose speeches did much to inspire the country in the dark days of 1940 when Britain faced possible invasion by Nazi Germany. At the end of the war, Churchill decided to call a **general election**. The last election had taken place in 1935 and Churchill believed that a new government should be elected to govern the country after the war. Most people expected Churchill to sweep to victory. However, even though people admired Churchill, they disliked his Conservative Party. The Conservatives had been in power for most of the time before the war and were blamed for the high unemployment and widespread poverty. Many people believed they had failed to prepare Britain properly for the war.

AND NOW – WIN THE <u>PEACE</u>

Labour printed posters asking people to vote for them in the 1945 general election.

🐾 What does the V stand for on the poster (above)?

DETECTIVE WORK

Britain has had 12 different prime ministers since 1945. Find out who they are, and which political parties they led, on http://www.number-10.gov.uk/output/Page123.asp

'We thought we were going to win, most of us, but by that margin? I doubt if anyone dreamed that we would win like that. I shall never forget the Forces' votes being tipped out from their tins. They were all for me. Really almost every one for me. It was astounding. I remember too the enthusiasm, the passionate conviction.'

Christopher Mayhew was successfully elected a Labour **MP** in 1945.

Churchill toured bombed-out houses during the war.

The election took place on 5 July 1945, but the votes were not counted until 26 July to allow for the soldiers' votes from around the world to be brought home to be counted. The result was a sensation. The opposition **Labour Party** led by Clement Attlee won 393 seats, the Conservatives only 210, other parties 37. Labour had an absolute **majority** of 146 seats.

Clement Attlee became prime minister in 1945.

What was rationing?

During the war, the entire national economy was directed towards fighting and winning the war against Germany. Ships brought in much-needed military supplies from abroad, but they had no room to bring in food. In any case, shipping was under constant attack by German U-boats, so only essentials were carried by sea.

As a result, the only food available in Britain was what could be grown at home. Everyone who had a garden planted vegetables and fruit bushes, while public squares and parks – and even the sides of the road –

The journalist, JL Hodson recorded the introduction of bread **rationing** in 1946 in his diary:

'Bread rationing is historic. We avoided it in two world wars, we come to it after a year of peace that bears some resemblance to war in its hardships. Master bakers growl bitterly, housewives, already sorely pressed, must assume another burden. But I do not think it will be so troublesome and harsh … There will be households – mine is one – where the ration will be greater than we now eat, and we shall be able, so they say, to exchange the surplus for other 'points' to give us extra tinned meat, biscuits and so on.'

DETECTIVE WORK

You are in charge of cooking for your family tonight. Find out from http://www.bbc.co.uk/history/ww2children/ration/ration_intro.shtml what sort of meal you might be able to produce. The ration is for 1943, but it was much the same as in 1945 or 1946.

Ration books for food and clothes were issued to every family in the country.

Why did the government take over industry?

The Labour Party was in favour of the state control of the main industries and services, such as banking. It believed that if the state owned and ran industry, it could use the wealth that industry created to invest in new machines and jobs rather than benefit rich owners and shareholders. It could also use the profits to build new homes, schools and hospitals, and make sure people had adequate health care, sickness and unemployment insurance, and education. In this way, wealth could be redistributed from the rich factory owners and shareholders to the poor working people.

Nationalization or state control of industries and services, was not new, as the national electricity grid, the British Broadcasting Corporation (BBC) and London Transport had all been set up under state control before the war. The need to direct industry to produce war materials meant that almost every industry was under some form of state control during the war. However, bomb damage to the mines, railways and other industries was massive, and a huge programme of public investment would be needed to rebuild British industry and put Britain back on its working feet again. State control had helped Britain to win the war, so could it not also help Britain win the peace? Most people thought so, and had voted Labour in 1945 in large numbers so that the government could take over the running of industry.

The scale of what the Labour government achieved was massive. It nationalized the Bank of England, the coal mines, **civil aviation** and the

> '*I was asked by [prime minister] Attlee to go to the Ministry of Fuel and Power ... to nationalize the mines. He also asked me to nationalize the electricity supply and gas. I went back to my department and consulted with my officials. Naturally, I looked around for some information, for blueprints, but there were none in the department. I went to the Labour Party; there was very little there ... so I had to tackle it as if it was something quite new. It was very difficult indeed to do it.*'

Emmanuel Shinwell MP remembers nationalization.

THIS COLLIERY IS NOW MANAGED BY THE NATIONAL COAL BOARD ON BEHALF OF THE PEOPLE JANUARY 1ST 1947

The coal mines were taken into public ownership in 1946.

Mothers often collected bags of coal and carried them home in a pram or a pushchair.

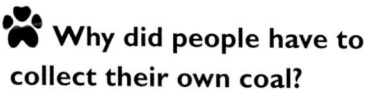 Why did people have to collect their own coal?

cable and wireless network in 1946, electricity supply in 1947, railways, road transport, docks, canals and the gas industry in 1948, and the iron and steel industries in 1949. Private ownership was replaced by state control exercised through a board of state-appointed directors. Direct workers' control of the industries was ruled out, and much of the previous management continued as before. Some workers were surprised to find that their old bosses were still in day-to-day control and that little, if anything, changed that much. But the idea that the people owned the coal mines or railway trains was a huge advance, as for the first time a government set out to alter the shape and purpose of society itself.

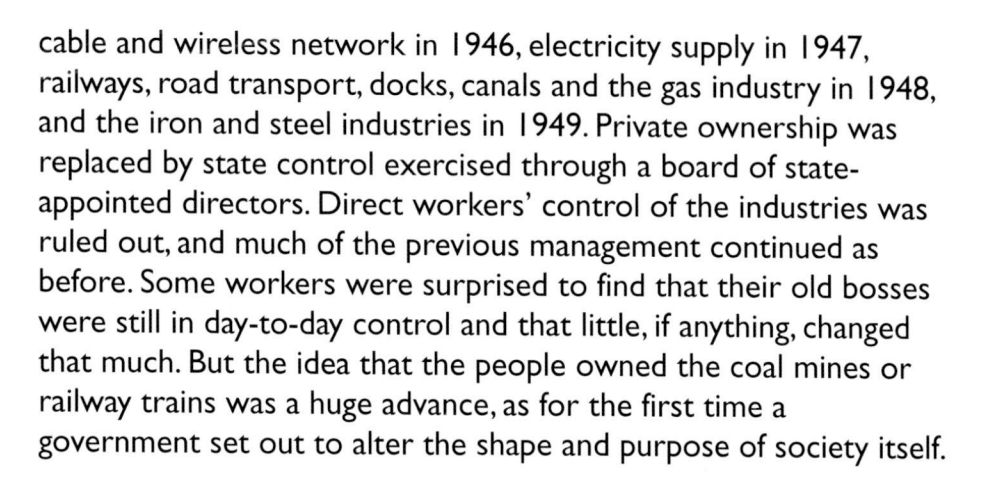

The Bank of England came under state control in 1946.

What was the welfare state?

The Labour government of 1945 believed that one of the most important tasks of the state was to prevent poverty and maintain an adequate standard of living for everybody. This meant not just making sure working-age people had jobs, but also looking after them if they were unemployed or injured through work. It also meant caring for everyone if they were poor or sick or in need. This sort of state is known as a welfare state.

'"The object of government in peace and in war is not the glory of rulers or of races, but the happiness of the common man." To achieve this happiness, he identified five dragons that needed to be slaughtered: *"Want is one only of five giants on the road of reconstruction ... the others are Disease, Ignorance, Squalor and Idleness."'*

Sir William Beveridge was very clear about the role of a modern government in his report *Social Insurance and Allied Services* (1942), commonly known as the Beveridge Report.

Sir William Beveridge provided plans for a welfare state after the war.

The man in the centre of this photograph is Aneurin Bevan, the Labour government minister who introduced the National Health Service.

The **welfare state** offered a wide range of welfare payments, including old age **pensions**. Unemployment and sickness benefits already existed, but usually only the poorest people qualified for help, and delivery was often split between national and local government and voluntary organizations. Many people received no help at all. The Labour government decided to reform the whole system. Its **blueprint** was a report produced in 1942 by Sir William Beveridge, an economist and social reformer. He proposed a comprehensive system of health and unemployment insurance and pensions for the elderly and widows, as well as a wide range of other benefits. His system was designed to look after everyone 'from the cradle to the grave'.

A start was made in 1944, when a new Education Act raised the school leaving age from 14 to 15 and provided free secondary education for every child (primary education was already free). Family allowances were first paid to mothers in 1945. A comprehensive national insurance scheme to cover unemployment, sickness, maternity and widows' benefits and old-age pensions followed in 1946, and a national assistance scheme providing cash payments for those in real hardship in 1948. The showpiece of this new welfare state was the National Health Service (NHS), introduced on 5 July 1948. This new service took over all existing voluntary and local authority-run hospitals and provided free doctors, medical treatment, hospital care and dental and eye services. Costs for this and other parts of the new welfare state were met through taxation and by compulsory contributions from both employers and workers.

DETECTIVE WORK

Find out more about your local hospital: how many doctors and nurses work there, what treatments and services does it offer, and how many patients does it care for? You could also find out about your local doctors' surgery and the services it offers. You will be surprised just what is available on the NHS!

What was the Festival of Britain?

After six years of warfare, and then six years of reconstruction, Britain was exhausted. Its people had had enough of rationing and other hardships and wanted entertainment. They wanted to celebrate their achievements, so the government decided to hold a huge, national Festival of Britain.

Herbert Morrison, the deputy prime minister to Attlee who was in charge of the event, proposed that 'we ought to do something jolly ... we need something to give Britain a lift.' He saw the exhibition as 'the people giving themselves a pat on the back.' The date chosen, 1951, was exactly 100 years after the Great Exhibition, which itself had been a huge celebration of British industrial and imperial greatness. The new festival was designed to imitate it, to show off British scientific, industrial and artistic skills to the world.

The main exhibition was built on an area of bombed-out warehouses and other buildings on the south bank of the Thames in London, almost opposite the Houses of Parliament. Other permanent and touring exhibitions – one of them on board a ship – took place around the country, while a huge fun fair was erected in Battersea Park, upriver from the main festival

DETECTIVE WORK

Visit the South Bank in London and see what is left of the Festival and its buildings. You might find this website useful: http://www.museumoflondon.org.uk/archive/exhibits/festival/index.htm

A special catalogue was printed listing all the events in the Festival of Britain.

Crowds flocked to the Festival of Britain every day it opened.

![Festival Guide To London illustration]

Festival Guide To London

The Festival spread out across the whole of London.

site. Every community in the country was encouraged to participate, and millions of people came to London to visit the main exhibition itself, many of them visiting the capital for the first time ever.

The exhibition site included a purpose-built concert hall – the Festival Hall – and 42 temporary pavilions used for exhibitions and shows, the main one of which was the 110 m (365 ft) in diameter Dome of Discovery. The site was filled with sculptures, mosaics and wall paintings and was dominated by the Skylon, a 90 m (300 ft) luminous exclamation mark pointing to the skies and held up as if by magic by a few thin wires. Numerous cafes and restaurants provided everyone with food and drink.

Many people criticized the Festival as a waste of public money – it cost £8 million – but it was a great success, with more than 10 million people visiting the South Bank and other festival sites, and another 8 million people having fun at the fair in Battersea.

'I was 15 years old just started working in the sign writing shop for this firm Mercury Display who had contracts to carry out exhibition and displays for the Festival of Britain. Fellow workmates and l had the job of completing the large Festival logo signs that would be on display round London. We had so much work to finish on time we worked seven days on 12 hours a day. My dad worked for the firm as a painter and worked mostly on site in the Dome of Discovery. We carried out many display signs in the Battersea Pleasure Gardens. My mum and dad took me to the exhibition and all l kept saying to them and pointing "l helped to do that".'

Ken Harvey had just left school when the Festival of Britain opened.

Were people better off by the 1950s?

During the 1950s, a new mood of confidence swept the nation. Most people were getting richer. The future looked bright but were the British people right to be confident?

Queen Elizabeth II was crowned queen on 2 June 1953.

Where is the king or queen crowned?

In 1952, King George VI died and was succeeded by his 25 year old daughter, Elizabeth II. Her **coronation** in June 1953 was a splendid **pageant**, watched on television by people all over the world. Britain now had a young, attractive queen and many people looked forward to being part of a new and glamorous Elizabethan age, just like the one the country had enjoyed under her predecessor, Elizabeth I, 400 years before. Politically, the Labour government had lost power in 1951 and been replaced by a Conservative government led first by Winston Churchill and then, after 1955, Anthony Eden. Eden resigned in 1957 because of ill health and was succeeded by Harold Macmillan, a clever political operator who led the Conservatives to a massive election victory in 1959. The newspapers called him Supermac, because everything he touched was a great success.

Most people were better off in the 1950s. The economy was doing well, so most people had a job. Incomes were rising and rationing had finally ended in 1954, so goods were now available in the shops and people had the money to spend on household items such as a television or washing machine or perhaps a small family car. The terrible housing shortage caused by wartime bombing was tackled as more than 300,000 new council houses were built each year. New towns sprung up around the country, the first motorway – part of the M6 in Lancashire – opened in 1958. Jet travel was now possible and more people were now spending their holidays abroad for the first time.

Yet all was not well in the 1950s. Much of British industry was old and inefficient, and needed huge investment in new machines and working practices. Germany and Italy, both of which had been defeated in the war, and France, which had been occupied, were now powering ahead of Britain in the economic league tables, and their citizens were far richer than most Britons. Despite the welfare state, many people were still poor or badly housed. The country still also had a social and political system based on privilege and class or status, with much power still in the hands of a few, rich landowners and those who had been educated in the better public (confusingly, privately as opposed to state-run) schools. Although the country was getting richer, not everyone was sharing in its wealth and success.

'Let us be frank about it, most of our people have never had it so good.'

On 21 July 1957, Prime Minister Harold Macmillan spoke at a Conservative Party rally in Bedford. He summed up the economic situation of the country.

Harold Macmillan was prime minister from 1957 to 1963.

Many people still lived in prefabricated houses erected to replace houses bombed during the war.

What happened to the British Empire?

In 1945, Britain still controlled the largest empire the world had ever seen. At its height it had covered more than one-fifth of the world's land and contained about 410 million people, one-fifth of the world's total population. Within 40 years, almost the entire empire had gone. So what happened to make it disappear so fast?

The **empire** had largely been acquired through conquest, and many of its people disliked British rule and wanted to rule themselves. Nationalist groups sprung up in most countries demanding independence. British military power was also severely overstretched after the war, and the country could not afford to keep large numbers of troops around the empire. Britain, therefore, began to prepare the empire for independence.

In 1945, the Labour government came to power with a pledge of home rule for India. This was achieved in 1947 when the two states of India and Pakistan (including what is now Bangladesh) became independent. Sri Lanka and Burma followed in 1948, as did Israel.

During the 1950s, the British government prepared black African nations for independence. In 1957, Ghana became the first independent black African state, followed by Nigeria in 1960 and the rest of Britain's African **colonies** by 1968. Malaya gained independence in 1957, and was merged with other former colonies, including Singapore, in 1963. In the West Indies, Jamaica and Trinidad became independent in 1962. Most of the smaller Caribbean, Indian and Pacific Ocean islands then gained their independence by the mid-1980s. The path to independence was not always straightforward, as many British settlers were fearful of their future in an independent state. In Rhodesia a minority white government illegally declared independence in 1965 and only accepted majority black rule as Zimbabwe in 1980.

At midnight on 11 December 1963, the British colony of Kenya became an independent state within the Commonwealth.

DETECTIVE WORK

Find out which countries used to be in the British Empire and when they got their independence. You will be surprised how many countries Britain once owned or ruled! This website will help you: http://freespace. virgin.net/andrew.randall1 /britempire.htm

In 1960, the British prime minister Harold Macmillan addressed the South African parliament and warned them that a 'wind of change' was blowing through the continent, bringing in black majority rule.

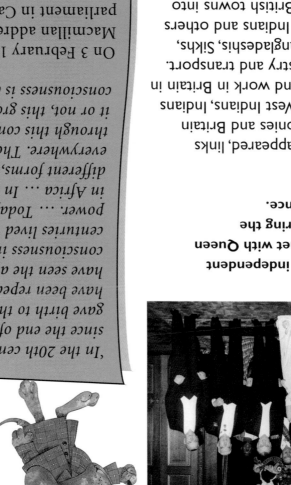

'In the 20th century, and especially since the end of the war, the processes which gave birth to the nation states of Europe have been repeated all over the world. We have seen the awakening of national consciousness in peoples who have for centuries lived in dependence on some other power. ... Today the same thing is happening in Africa ... In different places it takes different forms, but it is happening everywhere. The wind of change is blowing through this continent, and, whether we like it or not, this growth of national consciousness is a political fact.'

On 3 February 1960, Prime Minister Harold Macmillan addressed the South African parliament in Cape Town. He spoke about the changes facing Africa, as black African nations gained their independence, but he also warned the white South Africans that they too must change. It was not until 1994 that democratic elections were held in South Africa in which its black citizens could vote.

Although the empire disappeared, links between the former colonies and Britain remained strong. Many West Indians, Indians and Pakistanis came to find work in Britain in the health services, industry and transport. Large communities of Bangladeshis, Sikhs, Punjabis, Gujaratis, West Indians and others have transformed many British towns into multiracial and multi-religious communities.

In 1960, leaders of the 11 independent Commonwealth states met with Queen Elizabeth II in London during the Commonwealth Conference.

Which flag is being lowered and which flag will replace it in the picture on the opposite page?

Who were the teddy boys?

In the 1950s, a new generation emerged. These were the teenagers, a group of people not really identified before. Previously children had just grown up to become adults with no stage in between. In the 1950s, however, a new youth culture sprung up with its own style and values, as teenagers now had money of their own, and music and clothes to spend it on.

Two groups of young people made the headlines in the 1950s. The first were the beatniks, a mainly middle-class group who modelled themselves on the American 'beat generation' of poets and musicians. The beatniks wore black polo-necked sweaters, shapeless jumpers, long scarves and duffle coats, the men often had beards, and women wore black make-up. The beatniks liked modern jazz and literature and folk music and set out to be 'hip' and 'knowing', rather than 'square'.

The other group were the teddy boys. These were mainly working-class kids who wore clothes very loosely modelled on those of the Edwardian era. The men wore long, colourful drape jackets, narrow drainpipe trousers and crepe-soled shoes known as 'brothel creepers', while the women wore wide skirts tightly gathered in at the waist. The men wore their hair in a quiff fixed in place with Brylcreem; the longish sides were slicked back and met in the middle, a feature known as a 'duck's arse'!

The teddy boys originated in south London but hit the national stage in 1956 when a new form of music, Rock and Roll, first arrived from America. Elvis Presley entered the British charts six times that year, while the film *Rock Around The Clock*, featuring Bill Haley and the Comets, caused teddy boys to riot at British cinemas. Both beatniks and teddy boys hung out at coffee shops, as

DETECTIVE WORK
Find out more about the music the beatniks and teddy boys enjoyed. Older members of your family might have been young in the 1950s: ask them about their musical memories, as they might still have records from that time.

How did the teddy boys get their name?

A group of mainly women fans await the arrival at London airport in 1957 of their hero, Bill Haley.

This poster advertises the film Rock Around The Clock.

most were too young to drink in pubs and there were no nightclubs in those days that played their sort of music. The main attraction of a coffee bar was not its drink but its jukebox, which played the latest American music. Both groups despised the safe, tame music of their parents and the conservative attitudes they held.

A group of teddy boys were photographed on the seafront at Lowestoft in 1962.

Why did the 1960s swing?

During the 1960s, Britain led the world in music and fashion. The country had become bolder and more confident in itself, and young people had the energy and enthusiasm to do things for themselves. At the centre of this explosion was London, the swinging capital of the world.

Fashionable London revolved around the King's Road in Chelsea and Carnaby Street in Soho. Here boutiques sold cheap but fashionable clothes for both men and women. Previously, men used to dress very conservatively, in suits and ties or dull-coloured jumpers, but now they wore bright flowery shirts, hipster trousers, waistcoats and had long hair. Women wore mini skirts and other clothes modelled by Twiggy and Jean Shrimpton, the most fashionable models of the time.

During the 1960s, it cost 2d (less than one penny today) to get a mini skirt dry-cleaned.

Carnaby Street in London's West End was the most fashionable street in swinging London.

🐾 Why is the shop painted in such bright colours?

Housewives queue to get
a ration of potatoes for
their family.

were dug up to create vegetable gardens. In order to prevent food
shortages, and make sure everyone had their fair share of food, a
system of rationing was introduced. Every family was issued with a
ration book and given coupons that they could exchange for a
small weekly quantity of sugar, butter, bacon, meat and tea. Other
products were paid for as usual with money. This system stopped
the well-off people buying up all the available food and made the
distribution of food fair.

Weekly personal rations changed from year to year as new items
were added, or removed, from the list. The ration for May 1945
consisted of 8 oz (225 g) each of sugar and fats, 4 oz (112 g) each
of jam and bacon, 2 oz (56 g) each of cheese and tea, 2 pints (1
litre) of milk, and 1 egg. Six points were also awarded to use for
extra foods, such as biscuits, cereals and tinned soup if any of them
were available, and 3 points for chocolates and sweets. The food
provided meant that diets were not very interesting. The cook,
usually the mother of the household, had to be very creative when
planning a meal. However, rationing allowed workers to have a
better diet and provided school children with free school milk and
vitamins, with the result that many poor families ate better during
and after the war than they had in the 1930s.

Post-war rationing was necessary to ensure a fair deal for
everyone. However, people tired of endless queueing to get
coupons and then food, and wanted something better than the
drab and dreary meals that resulted. As the country recovered
from the war, and slowly got richer, rationing was ended for many
goods, finally coming to an end in July 1954.

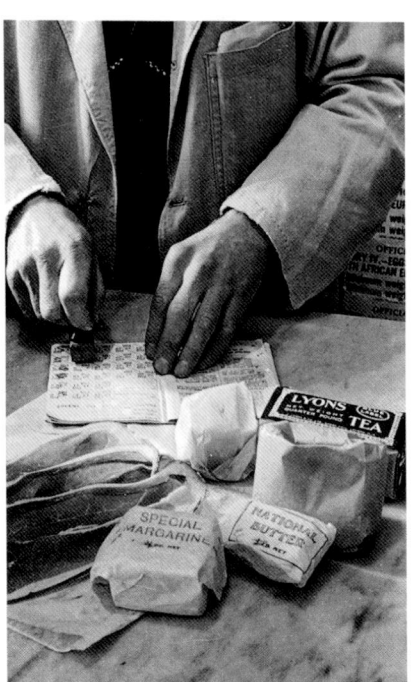

This shopkeeper is stamping a
customer's ration book.

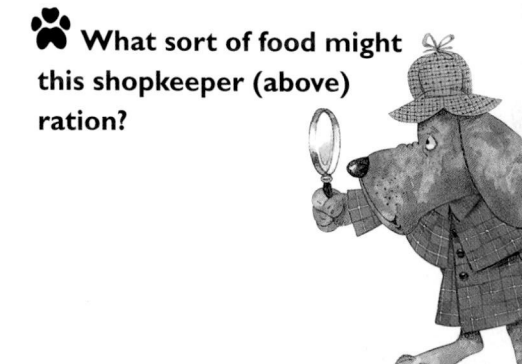

What sort of food might
this shopkeeper (above)
ration?

DETECTIVE WORK

Many people still consider the Beatles to be the greatest rock group ever. You can find out more about them and their music on their official website: http://www.beatles.com

The Beatles, starring from left to right Paul McCartney, George Harrison and John Lennon, with Ringo Starr on the drums.

'In this century, every decade has its city. Today it is London, a city steeped in tradition, seized by change, liberated by affluence, graced by daffodils and anemones, so green with parks and squares that, as the saying goes, you can walk across it on the grass. In a decade dominated by youth, London has burst into bloom. It swings; it is the scene.'

In April 1966, the American news magazine *Time* ran a cover story with the headline, *London: The Swinging City.*

The music to accompany this fashion revolution was dominated by the Beatles, a four-man group from Liverpool. Their first record, 'Love me Do', was a minor hit at the end of 1962, but the next year Beatlemania erupted as the Beatles started a run of best-selling singles and albums that continued until they disbanded in 1970. When they took America by storm in 1964, they led a flood of British acts that dominated rock music for years.

As fashion and music changed, so too did society itself. **Censorship** ended in the theatre and was beaten away in literature when in 1960 a charge of obscenity against Penguin Books for publishing DH Lawrence's novel *Lady Chatterley's Lover* was thrown out of court. New television programmes mocking or mimicking politicians and even the royal family became hugely popular. The contraceptive pill first became available in 1961, capital punishment was ended in 1965, abortion and homosexuality were legalized in 1967, and society as a whole became more tolerant and far more relaxed than before. In 1966, England even won the football World Cup for the first and only time, contributing to the feeling that Britain was indeed the best place to live in the world!

Why did Britain join Europe?

As Britain got rid of its empire, it found itself gradually isolated in the world. The US politician, Dean Acheson, famously said in 1962 that Britain 'has lost an empire and has not yet found a role'. Many politicians, therefore, looked towards Europe to secure Britain's future in the world.

After the war, leading politicians in France and West Germany (as it then was) began to plan a new future for Europe. Their two countries had gone to war three times in 70 years, but they now resolved to work together for peace and unity. In 1952, both countries, with Italy, the Netherlands, Belgium and Luxembourg merged their coal, iron and steel industries. In 1957, the six expanded this community into a far wider economic association based on free trade and joint social and financial policies when they signed the Treaty of Rome, setting up the European Economic Community (EEC), better known as the Common Market.

The European flag.

The British prime minister Edward Heath signs the treaty of accession that took Britain into the European Community in 1973.

DETECTIVE WORK

The European Union started with six members, but how many countries are members today and how many more want to join? Find out more about the European Union on http://europa.eu/abc/index_en.htm

Britain did not join the EEC when it was first founded. It soon became obvious that the union was a great success and was bringing increasing wealth to its member nations. In comparison, Britain was getting poorer. British industry needed to sell its products to Europe in order to survive, but could not easily do so if Britain continued to remain outside the EEC.

In 1961 and again in 1967, the British government applied for membership. Both times, the application was vetoed by the French president, General de Gaulle, who believed that Britain was too pro-American and not sufficiently pro-European. After de Gaulle resigned in 1969, British entry to the European Community (EC), as it was now called, became possible. After lengthy negotiations, Britain, under the Conservative government of Ted Heath, along with Ireland and Denmark, joined the EC in 1973.

The European Parliament has directly elected representatives from each member state.

Membership of the European Union, as it is called today, has brought many benefits to Britain, but is still a controversial topic for the British public. In 1975, the Labour government renegotiated entry terms: in the first and only **referendum** ever held in Britain, membership was approved with 67% in favour. Yet many people still dislike the EU and feel that British independence and culture are threatened by increasing moves towards full European union.

What was the 'Winter of Discontent'?

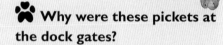

A massive rise in the cost of oil in 1973 led directly to a steep rise in inflation, a rise in prices, throughout the 1970s. Workers put in large wage claims and went on strike and refused to work if they did not get them. In 1978–79, the country almost ground to a halt in a period known as the Winter of Discontent.

In 1973, war between Israel and its neighbouring Arab states caused the Arab oil producing nations to raise the price of oil by 70% and refuse to sell any oil to the USA in protest at its support of Israel. Everyone around the world now had to pay much more for their petrol, causing a huge jump in the overall cost of living. Workers put in claims for huge pay rises to keep up with prices, causing prices to rise yet higher. Many of the workers went on **strike**.

🐾 **Why were these pickets at the dock gates?**

Pickets keep warm outside Felixstowe Docks as they prevent lorries entering and leaving the port in January 1979 during the Winter of Discontent.

In December 1973, prime minister Edward Heath put Britain on a three-day working week to ration oil supplies and energy. As a wave of strikes continued he then called a general election in February 1974 on the issue of 'Who runs Britain?, the government or the **trade unions** representing the workers?' He narrowly lost to the Labour Party under Harold Wilson. By August 1975, inflation had reached 26.9% a year. A normal rate of inflation would be between around 3 - 5 %. The government reached an agreement with the trade unions to moderate pay claims and inflation started to fall to 10% a year. In 1978, this agreement fell apart as trade unions refused to agree to a national wage increase limit of 5%. In January 1979, lorry drivers went on strike for a 25% pay rise, disrupting food and petrol supplies. Local government workers followed, resulting in rubbish piling up in the streets and even the dead left unburied in local cemeteries. Patients were turned away from hospitals and schools closed because they had no oil for heating, and the railways ground to a halt as the railway workers went on strike.

It seemed as if the government had lost control of the country. This winter had particularly harsh weather, but unfortunately the Labour prime minister, now James Callaghan, was attending a conference on the hot West Indian island of Guadeloupe while his country shivered at home. A deal between the government and trade unions on St Valentine's Day, 14 February, brought the strikes to an end, but by then support for the government had completely collapsed, as no one thought they could govern the country any more.

Thousands of workers marched through London on 22nd January 1979 to demand higher pay.

When prime minister Jim Callaghan returned from Guadeloupe in January 1979, a newspaper reporter asked him about 'the mounting chaos in the country at the moment.' He replied:

'Well, that's a judgement that you are making, I promise you that if you look at it from outside, and perhaps you're taking rather a parochial [narrow or limited] view at the moment, I don't think that other people in the world would share the view that there is mounting chaos.'

The next day' edition of The Sun newspaper then displayed a famous headline: 'Crisis? What crisis? – rail, lorry jobs chaos – and Jim blames press.'

Uncollected rubbish piled up in Central London during the Winter of Discontent.

Why did the government change in 1979?

In 1979, the Labour government had been in power for five years. It then lost a vote of confidence in the House of Commons by one vote and had to call a general election. The voters took the opportunity to throw it out and vote in the Conservative Party. Why was there such a dramatic change?

LABOUR ISN' WORKING.

UNEMPLOYMENT OFFICE

BRITAIN'S BETTER OFF WITH THE CONSERVA

During the 1979 general election campaign, the Conservatives accused the Labour government of causing unemployment.

Throughout its period of office, the Labour government had had to deal with the effects of the oil price rise of 1973 (see pages 24–25). Prices rose steeply, workers demanded higher wages to pay for them, and numerous strikes broke out when the workers' demands were not met. The government seemed to have the situation under control in 1978 but then the agreement between it and the trade unions fell apart, leading to the Winter of Discontent. Many people criticized the government for its handling of the crisis, and voted against them in the general election.

DETECTIVE WORK

Margaret Thatcher was one of the most important prime ministers of recent years, but many people strongly disliked her and her policies. Find out more about her on http://www.number-10.gov.uk/output/Page126.asp

Margaret Thatcher became the first woman prime minister of Britain in May 1979.

In addition, there was a general feeling in the country that it was time for a massive change. The country was struggling from crisis to crisis, and the only answer the government had was to bring the unions into a close relationship with the government. But the trade unions were very unpopular because of the strikes they caused, another reason to vote against the government.

In 1975, the Conservatives had elected Margaret Thatcher, the first woman leader of a major political party. Unpopular at first, she soon gained respect for her strong views. She wanted to end government links with the trade unions and cut their powers to strike. Most importantly, she promised to reduce government spending and debt in order to reduce taxes to strengthen the country's economy. This package appealed to the electors as a way to stop the economic decline of the country.

The election was held on 3 May 1979. The Conservative vote rose by 3.2 million to 13.7 million votes, the Labour vote stayed at 11 million. The Conservatives swept into power with a majority of 43 seats in the House of Commons. They were to stay in power for the next 18 years.

Margaret Thatcher was unexpectedly elected leader of the Conservative Party in 1975, defeating the then leader Edward Heath. No one was more surprised than her. In 1970, she stated that:

'It will be years before a woman either leads the Conservative Party or becomes prime minister. I don't see it happening in my time.'

Your project

By now you should have collected enough information about Britain in the years after the end of World War II. This is the time to think about the sort of project you might like to put together.

You might like to produce a profile of one of the main politicians that dominated this period of history, Winston Churchill, Clement Attlee, Harold Macmillan, Harold Wilson and Margaret Thatcher were all prime ministers during this time and did much to change Britain after the war. Try writing a short biography or life story of one of them, perhaps setting out events from their point of view and explaining why they acted in the way they did.

You could take part in a general election and draw up a **political manifesto** or statement of intent stating why you should be elected to parliament and asking the voters for their support. Pick a year in which the election is to take place, and then spell out what you believe is wrong with Britain and what you, as a candidate for the Conservative, Labour or Liberal Party, intend to do to set it right. If you don't want to write a manifesto, you could design an election poster instead. (See the examples on page 29.)

Harold Wilson was prime minister twice, from 1964-70 and again from 1974-76.

Alternatively, imagine that you live somewhere that was part of the British Empire, such as the Caribbean or India, and want to move to Britain. Make a list of all the reasons you want to move, as well as the reasons you might want to stay at home. Or you could imagine you were a worker about to go on strike for more pay or better conditions. Why do you want to strike and what do you hope to gain? What do you think you might lose if you did go on strike? Make a list setting out arguments for and against the strike, and why you should or should not take part in it.

You might have other ideas as to what project to do, but whatever you decide, it is your project, so choose something that interests you.

Project presentation

● Research your project well. Use the Internet and your local or school library. Is there a nearby society, museum or historical site related to your project? Many of these will also have their own Internet site.

● If you were a time-travelling journalist and could interview someone in this book, what questions would you ask them? Make a list, and then see if you can answer them from your research.

● Collect pictures about your subject and use them to illustrate your biography. You could also compile a list of useful websites and other sources of information.

A Conservative Party poster (right) and a Labour Party poster (below) show different ways a party can get its message across during a general election.

Glossary

bankrupt A person or company that owes more money than they can ever earn or repay and is officially declared insolvent or bankrupt.

blueprint An original plan or set of drawings that influences the finished design or practice.

censorship Policy forbidding or editing the production or performance of books, plays and films that are considered obscene.

civil aviation Passenger or freight air transport, as opposed to military aviation.

coalition Government formed with representatives from all political parties.

colonies Regions or countries controlled by another country.

Conservative Party One of the two major political parties in Britain, believing in private enterprise or business, the market economy, and a cautious approach to social reform.

coronation Act or ceremony of crowning a monarch.

Empire (British) Territories or peoples under the rule of the British monarch.

general election Election where parliament is dissolved and every member of parliament has to stand for re-election.

Labour Party One of the two major political parties in Britain, believing in state control of industry and services and a redistribution of wealth to achieve a fairer, more equal society.

majority (political) The number of MPs in the House of Commons voting for the government above the total number of MPs for the various opposition parties.

MP Member of Parliament.

nationalization A state take-over from private individuals of industry and services.

pageant Elaborate colourful parade or display.

pension Payment made to a person, usually weekly or monthly, after they have retired from work.

picket Person or group of people who attempt to influence or prevent others from working.

political manifesto A public written declaration of a political party's principles and policies.

rationing The system used in World War II that gave people a certain ration or amount of food per week.

referendum The submission of an issue of national importance to the direct vote of the people.

strike When workers refuse to work unless their demands are met for higher pay, better conditions, or shorter working hours.

trade unions Organisations of workers representing different parts of industry, such as railway drivers or coal miners.

vote of confidence Government or parliament pass a motion of support to show their confidence in the government.

welfare state A state that cares for the health and welfare of its citizens through state benefits, pensions, health care and other social measures.

Answers

Page 4:   V stands for victory.

Page 7:   Butter, margarine, bacon and tea were all rationed during and after the war.

Page 9:   Petrol was rationed after the war and there was a huge shortage of lorries and trucks to deliver coal, so people had to collect their own.

Page 14:   The king or queen is crowned in Westminster Abbey.

Page 17:   The Union Jack of Britain is being lowered and will be replaced by the flag of the newly independent Kenya.

Page 18:   Teddy boys loosely modelled their clothes on the Edwardian era before 1914, when Edward VII was king, hence their name.

Page 20:   Bright, psychedelic rainbow colours were very fashionable in the 1960s.

Page 24:   The lorry drivers' strike was unofficial, so some lorry drivers were still working and might try to get in or out of the docks. The pickets were in place to stop this happening.

Further Information

Books to read

When I was young: The Fifties by Neil Thomson (Franklin Watts, 2005)

When I was young: The Sixties by Neil Thomson (Franklin Watts, 2005)

I can remember: 1950s by Sally Hewitt (Franklin Watts, 2003)

I can remember: 1960s by Sally Hewitt (Franklin Watts, 2003)

I can remember: 1970s by Sally Hewitt (Franklin Watts, 2003)

Britain Since 1948: Home Life by Neil Tonge (Wayland, 2008)

Britain Since 1948: Popular Culture by Stewart Ross (Wayland, 2008)

Britain Since 1948: Work by Neil Champion (Wayland, 2008)

Websites

http://www.parliament.uk

http://www.museumoflondon.org.uk/archive/exhibits/festival/intro.htm

Note to parents and teachers: Every effort has been made by the publishers to ensure that these websites are suitable for children. However, because of the nature of the Internet, it is impossible to guarantee that the contents of these sites will not be altered. We strongly advise that Internet access is supervised by a responsible adult.

Places to visit

Houses of Parliament, Westminster, London, SW1A 0AA.

The South Bank, Belvedere Road, London, SE1 8XX – The original Festival of Britain was held here.

Index